MEDIEVAL FLUSHWORK
OF EAST ANGLIA

Further details of Poppyland Publishing titles can be found at
www.poppyland.co.uk
where clicking on the 'Support and Resources' button
will lead to pages specially compiled to support this book.

Medieval Flushwork
of East Anglia
and its Symbolism

BY

MARGARET TALBOT

POPPYLAND
PUBLISHING

Preface

Text set in 9 on 12 pt ITC Charter
Designed by Watermark, Cromer, NR27 9HL
Printed by Printing Services (Norwich) Ltd

To my son Ian Talbot
for all the hard work he did in gaining his PhD,
and also to my husband Glyn
for his encouragement in writing this book.

Those who have seen the flint motifs on the outer walls of the East Anglian churches cannot fail to have noticed how little mention they get in the majority of church guides, tourist guides or architectural literature. These flint motifs are unique pieces of artwork and have gone largely unnoticed by congregations and visitors alike.

The imagery is being eroded by weather conditions or cheap and insensitive repairs which have obliterated some of the fine details. There was a need for a visual record that would be of value to historians in the future. It is hoped that this book highlights the urgency of conserving these valuable images from the past.

Whilst recording the flushwork I had a desire for an explanation for their presence and to determine whether they were just decoration or had some deeper religious meaning – a difficult task after more than 600 years. The study of flushwork symbolism has proved to be a fascinating and enlightening experience.

There are many more motifs that have yet to be deciphered and future scholars may be able to suggest interpretations.

Contents

Elmswell

Worlingworth

Patterns in flushwork:

Laxfield

Stratford St Mary

Wortham and Cotton

Introduction

FLUSHWORK is a unique regional art form, given its name because the flint and stone are set flush with each other. Knapped flint and stone are combined to create architectural patterns and decorative motifs on the external walls of medieval churches. Although patterns in flint appear in other areas, Suffolk and South Norfolk have a peculiarly rich variety of symbolic designs. They appear on buttresses, parapets and string-courses (either low or high up), on clerestories and above porch doors. The art of flushwork has gone largely unnoticed by modern congregations and passers by.

The study of flushwork brings to life the way people thought in the 15th century, the political and religious structure of their society, their superstitions, beliefs and fears. It gives a true glimpse into the society before the Reformation and dissolution of the monasteries. This study includes pilgrimages, heraldry, trades, merchants' guilds and marks, the cult of the saints and above all the religious stranglehold on society in general. Religion was the framework of society. People did what the church wanted. At the time the Roman Catholic Church was dominant and the church was corrupt.

After the plague of 1349 came a labour shortage which gave more freedom of movement and ate away at the church's security. The rise in the cloth industry brought new wealth. At the same time, literacy was on the increase, and many people saw the value of learning to read in order to raise their place in society. (Perhaps this accounts for the alphabet in flushwork at Stratford St Mary church.) But the Bible was in Latin – there was no English translation for the ordinary folk. Tyndale translated the New Testament and had to flee the country because of it. He died in 1536, and the first printed English edition came out in 1540, fifty years after most of the flushwork was completed. The symbolism of flushwork would have been readily understood by a still mainly illiterate society. Medieval art was symbolic art symbolising the contemporary life and vision of heaven and earth that the medieval priests enjoyed. Symbolism was important then when the spiritual ideas represented were generally known and recognised and the meaning understood. Art was religious propaganda and until the late middle ages most art was religious in inspiration. Wall paintings, stained glass and carvings were used to inspire the faithful. Images were seen as a reflection of the glory of God. Very few of these survive today as they were almost completely destroyed when Henry VIII dissolved the monasteries in the 1530s. The flushwork has survived and is therefore an important part of pre-Reformation history.

The most striking feature of the East Anglian landscape is its enormous number of churches. Sometimes half a dozen church towers can be seen at once. A substantial number of Suffolk churches were built or remodelled after 1350, mostly financed from the wealth of the wool trade. Church building ceased by 1530. Over 400 medieval churches remain in Suffolk today.

Flint is the only usable local material for building in Suffolk. It is found in the fields and in vast quantities underground. Grimes Graves, near Thetford, have an area of 90 acres (36 hectares) with 360 flint mines. The field flints are encased in a thick layer of brownish chalk and are usually set into the walls whole. Knapped (split) flint is black and shiny like silk and it is not surprising that medieval craftsmen chose to use it artistically and to the glory of God.

Flushwork designs – patterns and motifs

Knapped flint was set into stone to create either a pattern or a motif. The patterns sometimes cover entire walls, or they form a string-course around the top or base of the church. The patterns are mostly diamond

Below left and centre: *Northwold*
Below right: *Ixworth*

or chequerboard sections or were inspired by architectural features such as window tracery and blank arcading. The illustration shows a few other patterns but this book is mainly concerned with the motifs and their interpretation.

The motifs are many and varied usually set into squares or roundels approximately 18 inches to three feet (45–90 cm) square. Religious beliefs or the requirements of benefactors to have their monogram, marks, heraldry or tools of trade immortalised in stone mostly inspire the representational designs. The non-representational motifs are either quatrefoils or mouchettes (curved dagger shapes) in varying numbers and arrangements. As a general rule the representational motifs are in stone on flint backgrounds and the non-representational designs are in flint on a stone background.

Symbols and their interpretation

In the 1400s the church used images to illustrate the principles of Christian faith for those who could not read. Our church buildings at that time were full of wall paintings, carvings and symbols that served as visual aids. A great deal has been written on religious symbolism, particularly of the Renaissance period, but information on pre-Reformation symbolism is widely scattered. A symbol represents or resembles something and has acquired a deeper meaning from that which is at first obvious. The interpretation of

BELOW LEFT AND RIGHT: *Northwold.* BELOW CENTRE: *Worlingworth*

symbols of early Christian art is often very difficult and a study of Christian texts does not always provide explanations. When, as with flushwork, we move from representation to abstract symbolism the problem of interpretation is doubled. The symbols can relate to the life of a person or an event and can be fact or legend. One must try to detect the Christian theological symbolism behind the arrangement of ornamental elements. Some ornament appears purely decorative, but detailed study has shown that the symbolism is extremely complex and subtle. Often the imagery is a coded reference to the benefactors who commissioned the work. The ostentatious inclusion of their name-saints was just the sort of pious swank medieval donors demanded as value for money and medieval artists loved a pun. I am convinced that flushwork incorporates a wealth of now lost meaning which is all the more complex to unravel because one symbol can serve to convey a variety of meanings. The explanations do not claim to be comprehensive, but represent our present state of knowledge.

Dating flushwork

Knapped flint rarely occurs before the 14th century and always remains a speciality of Norfolk and Suffolk. The earliest known flushwork is that of St Ethelbert's Gate in Norwich Cathedral Close (1316) and Butley Priory gatehouse in Suffolk (1311–32). The flushwork on the Suffolk churches dates from the 15th century, usually when the clerestories and towers were added and nave roofs were heightened during the major remodelling which was fashionable at that time.

The date 1499 in flushwork on the church at Stratford St Mary

Church	Flushwork Date	Number of Symbols
Bacton	1400–1500	40
Badwell Ash	1460–80	76
Blythburgh	after 1412	18
Cotton	after 1471	10
Elmswell	1476	86
Fornham All Saints	1450–1500	12
Gipping	1480	8
Grundisburgh	after 1418	12
Hawstead	1510	15+
Hessett	1450–1500	4
Horham	1499–1504	6+
Ixworth	1470	66
Lavenham (Stonework)	1486–1525	None in flushwork

Church	Flushwork Date	Number of Symbols
Mendlesham	1400–1500	27+
Northwold	1480–1500	98+
Rattlesden	1480–84	18
Rougham	1400–1500	10 + frieze
South Lopham	1460–80	4
Stratford St Mary	1494 & 1530	12 + alphabet
Walsham le Willows	1465	28
Woolpit	about 1450	14
Worlingworth	1400–1500	40+
Wortham	after 1410	19
Butley Priory	1311–32	Patterns only

Twenty-five churches were reviewed and 12 of these were dedicated to St Mary, so throughout the book I have referred to the church by its location to save any doubt as to which church is being referred to.

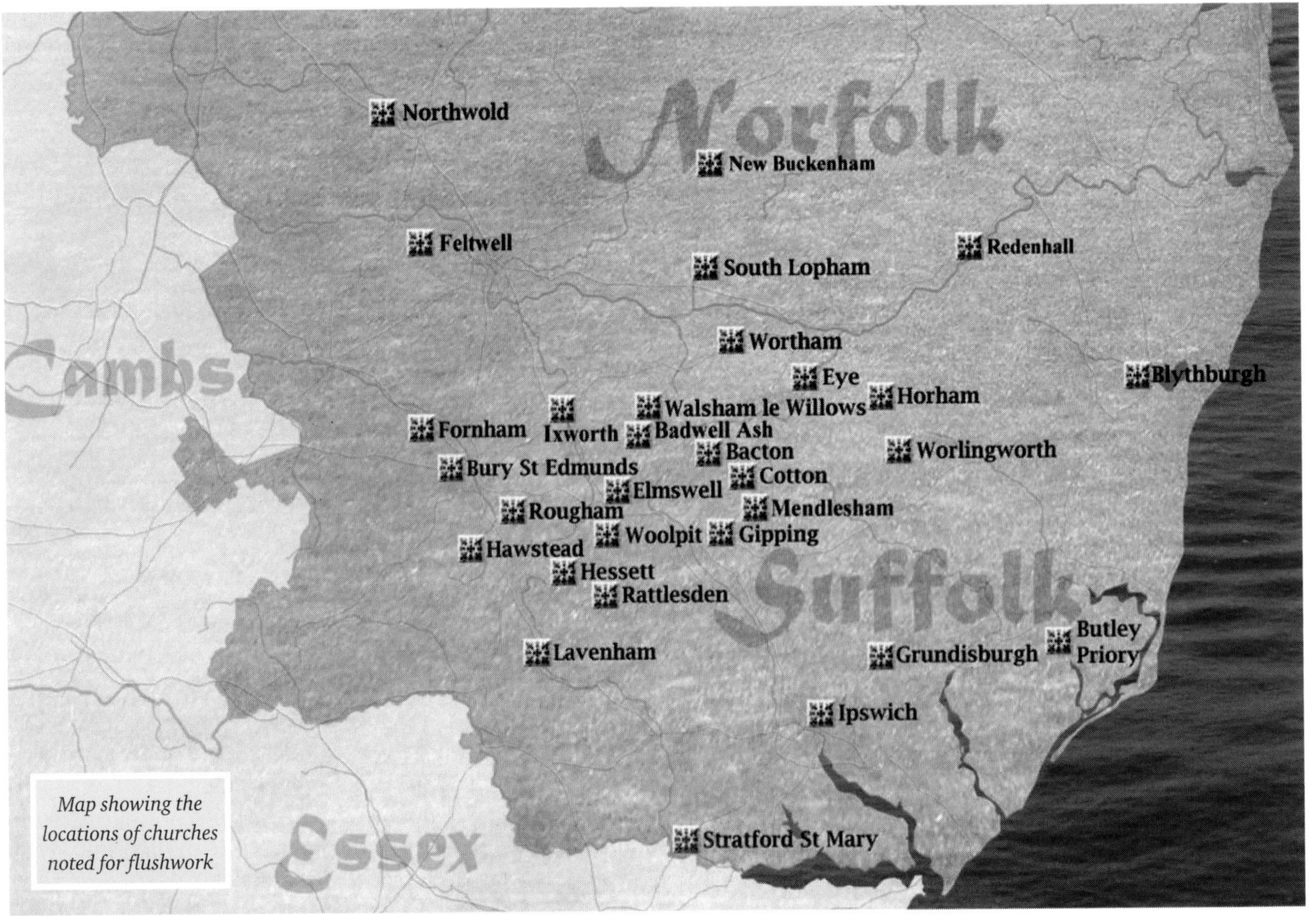

Northwold

Norfolk

New Buckenham

Feltwell

South Lopham

Redenhall

Wortham

Eye

Horham

Blythburgh

Cambs

Fornham

Ixworth

Walsham le Willows

Badwell Ash

Bacton

Worlingworth

Bury St Edmunds

Elmswell

Cotton

Rougham

Mendlesham

Hawstead

Woolpit

Gipping

Hessett

Suffolk

Rattlesden

Grundisburgh

Butley
Priory

Lavenham

Ipswich

Essex

Stratford St Mary

Map showing the locations of churches noted for flushwork

The Nativity – *The Glastonbury Thorn*

According to medieval legend, Joseph of Arimathaea, the Virgin Mary's merchant uncle, planted his staff in the ground on Glastonbury Tor, and it immediately

came to life and blossomed. Its mystique was unrivalled and it became famous across the land. Blossoming at Christmas time as well as in the spring, the Glastonbury Thorn became related to the day on which we celebrate the nativity of Jesus Christ. The thorn, *Crataegus oxyacanth* var. *Praecox*, is of a species which grows in the region of the Holy Land and the original may well have been planted by a pilgrim or crusader if not by Joseph himself. Legend has it that a fanatical puritan destroyed the original tree, but that another ancient thorn, a descendant of the original, stands at Glastonbury today. This image can be seen on Elmswell church tower buttress.

Epiphany – *The Star of the East*

The Star of the East, often seen in pictures of the Magi, was the star that guided the wise men to Bethlehem and stood in the sky over the manger where Christ was born. The church's season celebrating the Visitation of the Magi is Epiphany, which means the Manifestation of Christ to the Gentiles.

Traditionally this star always glows (has rays) as

Elmswell church: the Glastonbury Thorn

opposed to five- or six-pointed straight-sided stars. This symbol is only seen on Elmswell church.

Easter – *The Cross, Crown of Thorns and Palms*

Easter is the church's most important festival, celebrating the resurrection of Christ after he had been crucified. He wore a crown of thorns, which is one of the emblems of the passion and crucifixion of Christ. The palm branch is a traditional symbol of victory and martyrdom and is associated with Christ's triumphant entry into Jerusalem.

The Crucifixion – *Implements of the Passion*

The shield on Worlingworth church shows the objects involved in the passion of Christ, the cross, the lance, the whip, the sponge, the crown of thorns and the nails.

*Instruments of
the passion on
Worlingworth
church, and the
symbol of Pentecost
at Elmswell*

Northwold church has a shield with five circles which represents the five wounds Christ suffered while being crucified.

Pentecost – *The Tongues of Fire*

On Pentecost, in accordance with the promise of Christ that he would send the Holy Ghost to dwell in his church, the apostles were gathered in one place, and 'suddenly from heaven there came a sound like the rush of a violent wind, and it filled all the house where they were sitting. Divided tongues, as of fire, appeared among them, and a tongue rested on each of them. All of them were filled with the Holy Spirit' (Acts 2:2–4). In the paintings of Pentecost the Holy Ghost appears in the form of rays of light or flames.

This device appears only on Elmswell church. A close look reveals five white circles, possibly representing the marks of the Lord's passion.

The Resurrection – *The Wheel*

Wheels were quite a popular medieval image. The wheel appears on early Christian gravestones as a symbol of God and eternity. Most large rose windows are of the wheel construction. The number of spokes also plays a symbolically important role. The zodiac is frequently compared with the wheel (12 spokes) and

Wheels in flintwork at Badwell Ash

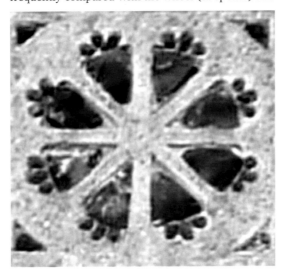

the last judgement. The eight-spoked wheel represents the wheel of life (most baptismal fonts are eight-sided) and this is the most common wheel in Suffolk flushwork. It sometimes surrounds a pommée cross (that is, a cross with ball shapes on the ends of the arms) of St Michael, the Archangel, the weigher of souls.

This image appears on Elmswell, Badwell Ash, Cotton, Walsham le Willows, Woolpit, Wortham, Bacton, Ixworth and Northwold churches.

The Trinity – *The Triangle and Circles*

The triangle and circles is the monogram of the Trinity, the three Persons in the one God, the Father, the Son and the Holy Ghost. Shown on the right is the doctrine of the Blessed Trinity. Trinity, one of the main festivals in the liturgical calendar, was the Sunday after Pentecost. The circles, two at the top next to each other and two in the centre below each other, on a shield, appear in flushwork on Northwold church. At Blythburgh the four circles on a shield are incorporated into the T for 'Trinitatis' meaning 'Trinity'. The Elmswell and Badwell Ash motifs have a large triangle incorporating the three circles.

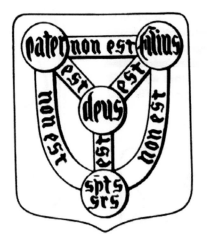

TOP: *Traditional diagram expressing the doctrine of the Trinity.*
BOTTOM ROW: *Symbols of the Trinity on churches at Northwold (LEFT), Badwell Ash (CENTRE) and Elmswell (RIGHT).*

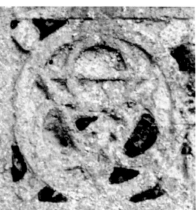

A chalice representing the Eucharist at Worlingworth, and FAR RIGHT foliage representing the season of Lent at Northwold.

The Eucharist – *The Chalice and Host*

A chalice is a cup from which the consecrated wine of the Eucharist is drunk at Holy Communion. The host is the flat, round piece of unleavened bread that the celebrant consecrates at the Eucharist, or mass. When shown with the chalice, it symbolises the sacrifice of Christ upon the cross. This emblem can be seen

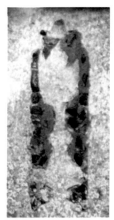

in flushwork at Badwell Ash (beside the main door), Elmswell, Worlingworth and at the end of the tower frieze at Rougham and in stone at Lavenham and Horham. This was not a particularly popular motif considering its significance as it only appears six times in the 25 churches that were visited.

Corpus Christi and Lent – *Foliage*

Corpus Christi Day celebrated the Eucharist and was held on the Thursday after the festival of the Trinity. It was marked by processions where the Holy Sacrament was carried through streets that were strewn with foliage. This was a very important festival.

The 6th Sunday of Lent is Palm Sunday that starts

Holy Week. It commemorates the solemn entry of Jesus into Jerusalem before his death on the cross. The congregation would meet somewhere outside the church to bless branches of boxwood or bay (instead of palms) before carrying them in procession around the church. Afterwards the faithful took home these branches which had been blessed and used them to decorate their crucifixes.

Foliage appears in flushwork on Bacton and Walsham le Willows churches and several times on Northwold church.

The Cult of the Saints

THE 12th and 13th centuries saw a tremendous religious revival in England and throughout Europe. People thought of the saints as intimate and trusted friends, involved in every aspect of life – and death – and, through their closeness to God, able to intercede on behalf of those on earth. Miracles were believed to occur frequently and many people were prepared to make long pilgrimages to shrines containing bones and other relics of the saints. There was a superstitious worship of images and relics, and the use of charms, amulets, potions, herbs and stones was commonplace.

In 1534 the Crown began to question many traditional religious practices. Lights before the many images in churches ceased. In 1536 an act was passed which limited holy days, resulting in the loss of many important saints' days. The year 1541 brought further refinements to the earlier act, reducing prayers for the dead and replacing prayers to the Virgin with verses from scripture. Henry VIII's Chantries Act of 1547 ordered the destruction of all images of the saints and abolition of all candles except before the sacrament. No saint was to be held to have a particular healing power and they lost their intercessionary powers and were demoted to mere moral examples.

English

St Edmund of East Anglia (841–69)
– Crown and arrows

The Abbey of Bury St Edmunds was built on the site of the shrine of the martyred Saxon King Edmund and rose to fame in the middle ages when St Edmund became the patron saint of England. King Henry VI (1422–71) prayed at the shrine of St Edmund at Bury.

Edmund was brought up as a Christian and became king of the East Angles. He was a humble man and strove to secure peace for his people. There was an invasion by the Danes and King Edmund was captured. He refused to deny the Christian faith and was killed. He remains the only English sovereign apart from Charles I to die for religious beliefs as well as the defence of his throne.

More than 60 churches in England are dedicated to St Edmund. His arms are shown with one crown and arrows on Rattlesden, Ixworth and Grundisburgh churches and three crowns and arrows (the arms of the Abbey at Bury) on Elmswell church.

St Edward the Confessor (1003–66)
– *The Letter E*

St Edward, King of England from 1042, was educated at Ely and was the founder of Westminster Abbey. He was devout and generous to the poor and loved peace. In the middle ages Edward was a very popular saint together with Edmund of East Anglia he was widely considered to be England's patron and was the patron saint of all Plantagenet kings. The Confessor's shrine at Westminster Abbey remains virtually the only medieval shrine to survive the English Reformation. St George's Chapel (begun 1475) at Windsor Castle is dedicated to the Blessed Virgin Mary, St George and

St Edward the Confessor. At least 17 ancient churches were dedicated to Edward. The flushwork on Elmswell Church shows a large E and a small d. Edward IV was on the throne at the time that the tower was started in 1476. The E also appears at Worlingworth and Ixworth Churches.

St Etheldreda – *A Necklace*

St Etheldreda, also known as St Audrey (died 679), was queen, foundress and abbess of Ely. She was the daughter of Anna, King of East Anglia, and was born in Suffolk. She remained a virgin during her two marriages and then became a nun and founded a double monastery in Ely in 673. Her shrine was much frequented and she became the most popular of the Anglo-Saxon women saints. The shrine at Ely was destroyed in 1541. Incidents from her life are carved on the capitals round the interior of the Ely Lantern Tower. Besides Ely, twelve ancient churches are dedicated to her. Her flushwork device appears on Rattlesden church as a crowned A on a saint's shield.

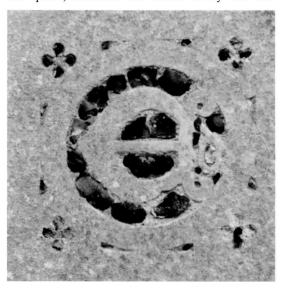

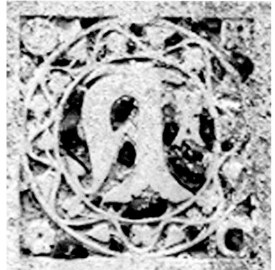

E for Edward at Elmswell, and A for Audrey (Etheldreda), surrounded by a necklace, at Northwold

On the buttress of Northwold church an A is placed within a necklace. She died of a tumour on the neck, interpreted as a divine punishment for her vanity in wearing necklaces in her younger days. At St Audrey's Fair necklaces of silk and lace were sold; these were often of so poor a quality that the word tawdry (a corruption of St Audrey) was applied to them.

St George, Patron of England – *The St George Cross*

St George was a 3rd-century martyr. His shield was the badge of the English from the days of Richard Coeur-de-Lion. It is for this reason these arms are borne by the Order of the Garter. In the 12th century the Templars used to call on St George to help them in battle.

The St George cross at Elmswell

In 1415 – the year of Agincourt, when Henry V invoked St George as England's patron – Archbishop Chichele had George's feast raised in rank to that of one of the principal feasts of the year. Edward the Confessor and Edmund of East Anglia were not entirely displaced, but George was a popular choice as a guild patron saint. St George's church at Stowlangtoft has very ornate chequerwork in flint on the porch, the stringcourse at ground level and on top of the tower. St Nicholas often replaced St George in a wave of rededications. Over 160 ancient churches are dedicated to him.

On Elmswell church there are two small devices on the porch and two large ones, but only one has a frill around the edge which could be a representation of the Order of the Garter.

Thomas of Canterbury – *The Letter T*

Thomas Becket (1118–70), archbishop and martyr, was born in London and became archdeacon of Canterbury in 1154, the year Henry II succeeded to the throne of England at the age of 21. He chose Thomas, at Archbishop Theobald's suggestion, as Chancellor of England in 1155. His personal efficiency, lavish entertainment and support for the King's interests – even, on occasion against those of the church – made him a quite outstanding royal official. In 1162 he became archbishop of Canterbury and deliberately adopted an austere way of life and immediately, to the King's annoyance, resigned the chancellorship. Becket was determined to carry through, at whatever cost, what he saw as the proper duties of his state. These included the paternal care of the soul of the King. Thomas opposed Henry in matters of taxation and the constitution. A long and bitter struggle followed and he escaped to France.

After six years Thomas returned to his diocese, but the reconciliation was superficial.

In defiance of the rights of Canterbury, Prince Henry had been crowned; Becket answered by excommunicating the bishops most concerned. In a rage Henry asked his courtiers who would rid him of this turbulent priest. Four barons took him at his word and killed him in his own cathedral.

The news of his death shocked Christendom. Miracles were soon reported at his tomb; within ten years they numbered 703. His faults were forgotten and he was hailed as a martyr for the cause of Christ and the liberty of the church. He was canonised in 1173. Representations of Becket's martyrdom rapidly appeared all over Europe; early examples survive

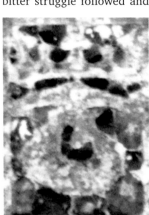  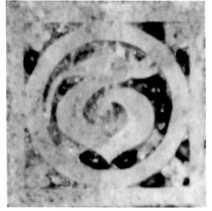

The letter T for St Thomas of Canterbury (Thomas Becket): LEFT *Stratford St Mary;* CENTRE *Wortham;* RIGHT *Ixworth*

not only from France and Germany but also from Iceland, Sicily and even Armenia. English murals were very common and 80 ancient English churches were dedicated to him.

In the 14th century the cult of St Thomas of Canterbury drew crowds of pilgrims on feast days and Jubilee years, but not the continuous pilgrimages there had been in the 12th century. His tomb, completed at enormous expense about 1220, astonished even seasoned travellers; it was adorned with gifts of indescribable beauty, including gold, silver and precious stones. When Henry VIII dissolved the Cathedral Priory the jewels and precious metals from his tomb filled 26 carts. Early in the 1500s, all mention of Thomas Becket was ordered to be removed from churches. This caused churchwardens to scratch his name out of their service books (as at Mildenhall) and to knock out windows (as at Bungay) and remove banners dedicated to the saint. The flushwork survived because of the difficulty in removing it.

In Henry VII's time (1485–1509), when flushwork was fashionable, Thomas was a popular guild dedication; thus the formal title of the Mercers' Guild is the Fraternity of St Thomas of Canterbury. Many churches in mid-Suffolk have the letter T in flushwork, including Elmswell, Fornham All Saints, Rougham, Badwell Ash, Mendlesham, Ixworth, Bacton and further afield at Stratford St Mary, South Lopham, Northwold, Felt-well and Blythburgh. Some of them show a crown above the T to indicate that he was a saint.

Foreign and Biblical

St Andrew – *The Cross Saltire*

According to tradition, St Andrew was crucified on an X-shaped cross (known as a saltire or St Andrew's cross) in Achaia. St Andrew (who died about AD 60) was an apostle and martyr, brother of Simon Peter and a fisherman. He was a disciple of John the Baptist before becoming an apostle of Christ. He is specially mentioned for his share in the feeding of the 5,000.

Churches were dedicated to him in England from Anglo-Saxon times and Hexham and Rochester were the earliest of 637 medieval dedications. The cross saltire appears in flushwork on Northwold church, dedicated to St Andrew.

St Catherine of Alexandria – *The Wheel and Spikes*

A wheel usually having eight spokes each ending in a curved spike represents St Catherine. She had studied much and converted many people, even the pagan philosophers whom the emperor sent to convince her

that Christianity was foolish. She refused to marry the emperor and he threw her into the dungeon. She continued to convert people and he decided she must die. A wheel set with razors was constructed and the saint was tied to the rim. Instead of cutting her to pieces, the wheel broke. She was finally beheaded.

St Catherine became one of the most popular saints of the middle ages and a favourite subject of artists and craftsmen. The discovery of her relics in the 9th century, and their removal to the Sinai mon-astery, began to attract pilgrims. Returning crusaders, travelling monks and pilgrims helped to spread the legend abroad, and her cult spread rapidly through-out Europe. This led to streams of pilgrims and travel-lers to her shrine in the next centuries and the monas-tery became the richest in Christendom.

In the later middle ages, chapels and churches were dedicated to her. She was widely adopted as a patron saint and is represented in innumerable paintings, icons, sculptures, wall paintings and stained glass –

in the 16th century, much remains although there are virtually no statues of St Catherine left in this country.

It seems probable that St Catherine never existed, but to the people of the middle ages she was very real. By the end of the 18th century doubt had been cast on the authenticity of St Catherine's life, and she was finally removed from the Universal Calendar of Saints in 1969.

Her wheel can be found in flushwork on Elmswell, Woolpit, Bacton, Wortham, Walsham le Willows, Ixworth and Northwold churches and several Lady chapels in this area were named after her.

St John the Apostle – *The Cup and Viper*

The emblem of St John, the 'Beloved Apostle', refers to the legend of the poisoned chalice. This was offered to him during captivity as a test of his faith. He was said to have charmed the poison out in the form of a serpent and then drank safely. He was released and became the first Bishop of Ephesus (now in Turkey).

John looked after Mary following Jesus' death. The cup and viper motif and the crowned M for Maria are placed one each side of the west tower doors at St John's church Elmswell and at Ixworth, Northwold and Mendlesham. These two symbols are usually placed near to each other. St John and Mary always appeared together at the foot of the Cross on Rood

often with the wheel, the symbol of her martyrdom. In 1473 St Catherine's college was founded in Cambridge and hospitals (for the elderly, the sick and for pilgrims) were founded in her name. Some 62 churches were dedicated to her, and 170 medieval church bells bear her name. St Catherine was the patron saint of the Haberdashers' Company in the city of London, which obtained a charter in 1448.

In Britain, where so much iconographic material was destroyed at the dissolution of the monasteries

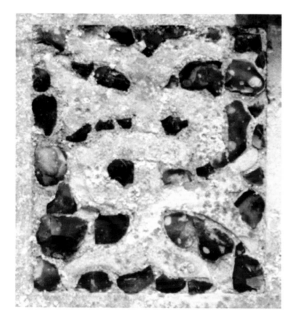

St John the Baptist – *The Maltese Cross*

St John the Baptist (1st century) was the last of the Jewish prophets of the Old Testament and the first of the saints of the New Testament. He prepared the way for the coming of Jesus Christ and performed many baptisms for the repentance of sins.

LEFT *The cup and viper of St John the Apostle at Elmswell*

John preached to the people near to the River Jordan saying, 'I baptize you with water; but one who is more powerful than I is coming; I am not worthy to untie the thong of his sandals. He will baptize you with the Holy Spirit and fire' (Luke 3:16).

This symbol appears on Elmswell, Badwell Ash and Wortham churches and twice each on Bacton, Northwold and Worlingworth churches.

BELOW: *The Maltese cross of St John the Baptist as depicted at* LEFT *Badwell Ash, and* RIGHT *Elmswell*

screens of this period. Medieval glass at Mendlesham shows St John holding a chalice.

Sometimes the emblem is a simple J with an interwoven S; occasionally the S is back to front. Often the J is chalice shaped and the S has serpent-like jaws and tail. At least twelve churches carry this symbol in flushwork: Elmswell, Bacton, Stratford St Mary, Wortham, Badwell Ash, Ixworth, Northwold, Mendlesham, South Lopham, Horham, Worlingworth and Feltwell.

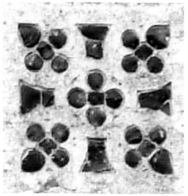

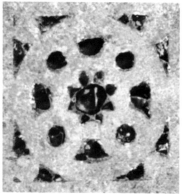

St Lawrence – *The Gridiron*

St Lawrence (died 258) was the archdeacon of Rome who, when ordered to deliver the treasures of the church to pagan authorities, produced the poor and sick of the Christian community as the richest treasures of the Church. He was condemned and burned to death over a gridiron; retaining his cheerful attitude to the end, Lawrence shouted 'I am roasted on one side. Now turn me over and eat!'

Before the Reformation English dedications numbered 228. The gridiron in flushwork appears on Elmswell, Hessett, Ixworth and Northwold churches. See the section on St Stephen.

St Stephen – *The Stones*

The stones refer to the manner of St Stephen's death (about AD 35). He was the first Christian deacon and the first martyr for the faith. His story is told in the sixth and seventh chapters of the Acts of the Apostles, where it is stated that 'Stephen, full of grace and power, did great wonders and signs among the people' (Acts 6:8). But those of the old faith in Jerusalem were angered by Stephen's words and by his influence over the people. They had him arrested and accused of having spoken blasphemous words against Moses and against God. He was taken out of the city and stoned to death.

Legend states that four hundred years after his

death, a priest in Palestine had a vision in which the resting-place of Stephen's body was revealed. As a result the relics of the saint were taken up and reburied in Rome beside the relics of St Lawrence, who allegedly moved to one side to make room. Because of the legend of this burial, St Stephen and St Lawrence are often portrayed together. This is the case on Elmswell church buttress where the gridiron for St Lawrence is directly above the saint's shield with the stones of St Stephen. Both motifs appear on Northwold church but on separate buttresses.

St Michael, Archangel – *The Pommée Cross*

St Michael was the leader of the celestial armies and guardian of the souls of men and was sent to announce to the Virgin her approaching death. From earliest times his cult was strong in the British Isles, reaching its peak in the middle ages. Pilgrims from all over Europe would embark on journeys to the major shrines such as St Michael's Mount, Cornwall or Mont St Michel in Normandy. Chapels to St Michael crown sites of ancient sanctity such as Glastonbury and Brentor. By the end of the middle ages his church dedications numbered as many as 686. St Nicholas often replaced St Michael at a later date. The cult of St Michael is older than the cult of St Mary, which grew up in the 12th century.

St Michael was believed to carry souls off to paradise and was said to be so powerful that souls could

The pommée cross of St Michael at Elmswell (LEFT AND RIGHT) and Northwold (CENTRE).

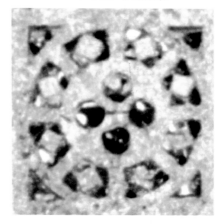

be rescued even from hell. His feast was called 'St Michael and All Angels' and was held on 29th September when the sun is in Libra, the sign of the scales of justice, when the hours of darkness and light are evenly balanced. When Michael is represented with scales or balances in his hand he is acting in his office as the weigher of souls. He is the patron of cemeteries. The pommée cross emblem is traditional, although the explanation is lost, and appears in flushwork on Elmswell, Badwell Ash, Blythburgh, Northwold and Worlingworth Churches. Northwold has flowers set into the circles and some crosses are set into a circle of eight squares, which is the number of new life.

All Saints and All Souls

Since the 9th century, 1st November has been a celebration of the memory of all the saints. The next day, 2nd November, is consecrated to All Souls. This celebration of the dead was founded by Saint Odilon (died 1049), Abbot of Cluny. The All Saints' shield and the Archangel Michael and doves panel (All Souls) appear at Elmswell and together on

The symbols of All Souls at Elmswell and All Saints at Hessett (RIGHT).

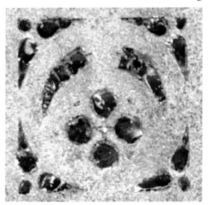
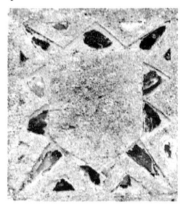

Northwold Church. Doves represent the Holy Spirit and also the souls of the faithful on their way to heaven.

Ancient English dedications to All Saints number 1,255, a number surpassed only by those dedicated to the Virgin Mary, whereas only four dedications to All Souls are known.

Christ and St Mary

Christ's monogram – *IHS*

A monogram is a motif composed of two or more letters, often interwoven, to produce a beautiful and symbolic design.

The use of groups of letters derived from Greek

and Latin words as symbols of our Lord Jesus Christ began in the early days of the Christian Church. IHS, JHS, IHC and XP (Chi-Rho) have all been used as Christ's monogram. Sometimes a crown is placed above the letters.

Twelve churches reviewed had Christ's monogram, compared with twenty for Maria. These churches are Elmswell, Rattlesden, Stratford St Mary, Wortham, Woolpit, Walsham le Willows, Fornham All Saints, Ixworth, Rickinghall Superior, Northwold, Horham and Worlingworth.

The Sacred Heart

The festival of the Sacred Heart was one of the main festivals in the liturgical calendar and was held on the second Friday after Trinity Sunday. It was based around the idea of Christ's human love for the world, and

The sacred heart at Elmswell

suggested by the episode during which his heart was pierced after his death on the cross. The water and blood

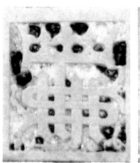   

The sacred monogram at (LEFT TO RIGHT) Ixworth, Rattlesden, Wortham and Worlingworth churches.

that flowed from that wound symbolise the sacraments, which spring everlastingly from Jesus' open heart.

This symbol appears only on Elmswell church, high up at the rear of the tower.

The Star of David – *A six-pointed star*

The Star of David in stone carving appears twice on the Great Gate of Bury Abbey, rebuilt 1335–53 after the uprising of the town in 1327. It also appears in flushwork on Elmswell (1476) and Northwold (1480) churches that came under the jurisdiction of the Abbey. (Both churches have similar flushwork.)

Jesus was traditionally thought of as the heir to King David and the great prophet whom Israel was awaiting (and whom the Jews are still awaiting today).

The star first came into popular use on Christian churches and hostelries in medieval times and also on buildings erected by the Knights Templar, who housed passing pilgrims. The motif was also a popular inn sign in medieval times, which suggests it was a symbol of hospitality. The Benedictine monks at the Abbey in Bury St Edmunds provided infirmaries offering refuge to the old and dying, as well as accommodation for travellers and pilgrims. St Benedict wrote, 'Let all guests who come to the monastery be entertained like Christ himself because he will say, "I was a stranger and you took me in".'

The Star of David at Elmswell

For 15 years (855–70) Edmund ruled over the East Angles with what all acknowledged as Christian dignity and justice. He seems to have modelled his piety on that of King David in the Old Testament, becoming especially proficient at reciting the psalms in public worship. Most monasteries recited all 150 Psalms every week, these being said or sung during the three or more services each day.

There is a Star of David on the book that Christ is holding in Giovanni Bellini's painting 'Christ Giving the Blessing' of the late 15th century.

*The Star of David
above the Great Gate
of the Abbey of Bury
St Edmunds*

St Mary – *The Monogram of the Blessed Virgin*

The M ingeniously incorporates each of the letters of the word MARIA or AMR. Maria was Christ's mother, Saint Mary, and AMR stands for 'Ave Maria Regina', which is Latin for 'Hail Mary Queen'. A crown was sometimes placed over the monogram by medieval artists which then symbolised the Immaculate Conception. At Mendlesham church the feast of the Assumption of Our Lady on 15th August is still kept as the patronal festival of the church.

The cult of St Mary sprung up in the 12th century with manuscripts collecting accounts of miracles. The Virgin as protectress of all pilgrims appears on many hat badges and tokens of that time. A tenth-century collection of blessings written for Bishop Ethelwold contains one of the first representations of Mary being crowned that survives in the West. All military orders of the 12th and 13th centuries claimed the Blessed Virgin Mary as a patroness.

At Ixworth and Fornham All Saints we see a twist in the centre stem of the M. During her cult St Mary was thought to be endowed with healing powers. A serpent entwined about a rod was the emblem of Asclepius, the Greek god of medicine. Fornham All Saints church was in the possession of the monks of the great Benedictine Abbey at Bury, and the ruins of a 12th-century hospital for elderly monks named St Saviour still stands in Fornham Road in Bury. Ixworth priory no doubt had accommodation for the sick.

Twenty out of the thirty churches reviewed had the St Mary monogram. Sixteen of those had a crown

The crowned M of St Mary as seen at (LEFT TO RIGHT) *Woolpit, Stratford, Elmswell and Ixworth.*

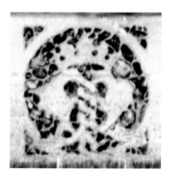

above the lettering. Twelve of these churches were called St Mary.

This symbol can be seen in flushwork on the churches of Elmswell, Badwell Ash, Woolpit, Rougham, Stratford St Mary, Wortham, Fornham All Saints, Ixworth, Bacton, Rattlesden, Gipping, Mendlesham, Blythburgh, South Lopham, Walsham le Willows, Rickinghall Superior, Northwold, Horham, Worlingworth and Grundisburgh.

The Virgin Mary – *The Mystic Rose*

Since the earliest years of Christianity the white rose has represented purity. The Virgin Mary is called a 'rose without thorns', because of the tradition that she was exempt from the consequences of original sin. On Elmswell church tower (1476) and Northwold Church it is placed next to the Maria symbol and at Ixworth tower (1470) it was placed between the 'T' for St Thomas and the IHS for Christ. The white rose must not be confused with the red rose that was adopted as a symbol of the triumphant house of Lancaster with the accession of Henry VII in 1485. The Tudor rose symbolised the union of the two rival families of York and Lancaster, who fought for the English throne during the Wars of the Roses (1455–85) and were united by the marriage of Henry Tudor to Elizabeth of York in 1486. The rose in flushwork is much too early to represent the House of Tudor.

The Mystic Rose appears on Bacton, Wortham, Walsham le Willows, Worlingworth, Elmswell, Northwold and Ixworth churches.

The Vase and Lilies – *The Virgin Mary*

The lily is a symbol of purity and has become the

The Mystic Rose representing Mary, as seen at (LEFT TO RIGHT) Worlingworth, Ixworth, Wortham and Northwold.

A vase with lilies, representing the Virgin Mary, at Grundisburgh (LEFT) and Elmswell (CENTRE). RIGHT: vases with lilies in a crowned AMR monogram at Rougham.

flower of the Virgin Mary. A vase holding a lily is one of the most frequently depicted objects in paintings of the Annunciation by the Archangel Gabriel and refers to Mary, the mother of God.

Elmswell church tower has quite a tall flushwork vase and lily standing alone. Below the battlements of Rougham church tower is a very large crowned Maria symbol incorporating two vases each with a single lily.

This motif also appears on Grundisburgh church between the clerestory windows.

Medieval life

Heraldry

The first heraldic devices were painted on shields about 1166 – they were bold, simple and symbolic designs. For centuries people have erected representations of the royal arms as expressions of their loyalty to the Crown or to commemorate a royal connection or benefaction. Local knights and officials who gave money for building the church would want their heraldry on the church for all to see. Since the 1400s the heraldry has been quartered (combined) and it evolves as families marry. Unless there is a reference to these early coats of arms on the brasses or memorials in the church their names may be lost.

At Grundisburgh church, the benefactor of the Lady Chapel, Thomas Wall, had no arms of his own so he had the arms of the Salters' Company (three salt cellars) and the arms of the City of London put one each side of his merchant mark on the parapet, showing that he was a citizen and salt merchant of London.

Three crowns and arrows, the arms of the Abbey at Bury St Edmunds, appear on Elmswell church tower.

Bourchier and Chamberlain heraldry, Rattlesden

A mitre and crossed croziers for Hervey, Bishop of Ely 1109–31, are on the eastern parapet of Rattlesden church and the arms of the Chamberlain and Bourchier families of Rattlesden are on the west parapet.

The gatehouse of Butley Priory (built 1311–32) has an extensive armorial frieze consisting of five rows of shields, seven to each row, alternating with panels of fleur de lys. The top row of shields represents the great Christian countries. The next two rows show the arms of the great baronial families of England – the de Veres, Bohuns, Beauchamps, Warennes and Clares. The last two rows represent East Anglian noble and gentry families.

Lavenham church porch was the personal contribution of John de Vere. Not in flushwork but deserving a mention, two boars immediately above the doorway are heraldic motifs (boar in Latin is *verres*). At the

base of each buttress flanking the doorway, there is a carved stone star, known armorially as a 'molet'. De Vere stars appear around the base of the tower (1486) and also on the walls higher up.

Thomas Spring III, the rich clothier of Lavenham, the wealthiest man in England outside the nobility, has his shield on the top of the tower (completed about 1525). He also has 32 shields on the parapet (carved in stone but no flintwork).

Hawstead church has flushwork pelicans and mullets on the top of the tower (completed around 1510) belonging to the Cullum and Drury families respectively.

St Nicholas' Chapel, Gipping, was the private chapel of Sir James Tyrell (restored 1480). The flushwork

The Tyrell knot at St Nicholas' chapel, Gipping

is almost entirely devoted to his family's monograms and badge except for a very small IHS and an M for St Maria set in double hearts in the flushwork patterning. In contrast his badge, the knot resembling the triquetra is large, and also set in a double heart, and surrounded by a wreath. Another device shows a large T intertwined with the knot of the Tyrells. Several other knots are carved in stone and one is set in six circles of knapped flint.

Inscriptions – *'Pray for the souls of . . .'*

Medieval people believed in the reality of purgatory, a place where the souls of the dead endured torment until their sins were expiated. Wall paintings uncovered recently depict the agonies of those in purgatory in terrifying detail, with the suffering dead crying out to the living for more prayers and masses. Christian concern for the dead is attested by the very many medieval bequests and chantry foundations.

The Cullum pelican and Drury mullets, Hawstead

*Inscription at
Rougham soliciting
the prayers of
the faithful for a
departed benefactor.*

Many wills bequeathed goods and money to the church to employ chantry priests to say mass for their soul after death and thus secure their speedy release from purgatory.

There are the remains of a medieval doom painting on the wall inside Bacton church. It shows the graves opening and the dead rising up on the Day of Judgement. The righteous are being received by St Peter (carrying keys) standing at the gate of heaven. The Seraph sends the wicked to the two devils who consign them to everlasting fire. Scenes such as these were commonplace but were lime-washed over during the Reformation. The object of these fearful pictures was to remind the illiterate church members of their ultimate destiny. Several rich merchants in Suffolk who were benefactors to their churches paid to have inscriptions put where all could see and would be reminded to pray for them in the afterlife.

Inscriptions to this purpose can be seen in flushwork on Rougham, Badwell Ash, Southwold and Stratford St Mary churches. At Badwell Ash the tower battlements were added about 1480. From the west the flushwork inscription reads: 'Pray for the good Enstat (i.e. wellbeing) of jon finchom and margit hys wyfe'. At Stratford St Mary, lower than the windows on the west wall of the aisle, facing the road, is a very large Latin inscription meaning 'Pray for the souls of Thomas Mors and Margaret his wife who caused this aisle to be erected in the year of our Lord 1499'. On the later Eastern part of the aisle at ground level in large flushwork lettering in English reads 'Praye for the soullys of Edward Mors and Alys hys wyf and all crysten sowlys Anno Domini 1530'. Below the tower battlements on the south side of Rougham church in letters

*An inscription on
Fornham church
beseeches Jesus to
have mercy.*

which can be clearly seen from the ground the inscription 'Pray for ye sowle of John Tillot' appears.

Fornham All Saints and St John the Baptist church at Needham Market both have a set of three flushwork panels that are almost identical with the general plea for one's soul that says 'Lord Have Mercy'.

Merchants' Marks

In the late middle ages almost every craftsman used a mark whether he was a trader or not. They are known to be in use in England as early as the end of the 13th century. There were masons' marks, paper makers' marks, marks placed on products by armourers, goldsmiths, pewterers, bell founders, coopers, glaziers, printers, bookbinders and other craftsmen. Marks can be seen on the ridgepoles of houses (as protective talismans), on brasses (earliest 1349) and grave slabs. Sometimes initials have been incorporated in a mark and some marks were used as signatures although the use of a mark does not necessarily indicate illiteracy. No one position was regarded as 'right way up'. Many marks were scratched on the woodwork or mortar of the church. Others were often displayed on a roundel, quatrefoil or shield. There is no concentration of marks except in East Anglia, Salisbury and the Cotswolds.

At Lavenham church, around the base of the tower, begun in 1486, are several merchant marks of Thomas Spring II of the cloth weaving family. His son, Thomas Spring III, who died in 1525, had his merchant mark used as full stops in the inscription on the southern side of the Lady Chapel. Both were benefactors of the church. Likewise Thomas Mors, another wealthy cloth merchant, had his trademark included several times on the north aisle of Stratford St Mary church in 1499.

Merchants' marks: LEFT TO RIGHT *Thomas Spring, Lavenham; Thomas Wall, Grundisburgh; Thomas Mors, Stratford; his son Edward Mors, Stratford.*

The embattled stone parapet (added in 1527) at Grundisburgh church has a merchant mark carved like a reversed 4 on a triangle showing that the Lady Chapel was a gift of Thomas Wall. His mark also appears several times within the church.

Tools of trade

Leather tanning

One of the forgotten industries in Suffolk is the processing of hides and skins. The work was more urban based than some other Suffolk industries as tanners required water.

From 1500 to 1750 Bury St Edmunds had more than 67 craftsmen and Ixworth possibly more than 20, Badwell Ash had several craftsmen preparing leather besides other workers who manufactured goods made from leather. Stowmarket had up to a dozen and Needham Market at least a dozen.

The flushwork image looks like a stretched and folded fabric with the tools of trade around the edge. Four tools are shown at Badwell Ash and one is clearly a knife. The Ixworth image has four different tools that include a mallet and a knife. At Rougham only two tools are seen crossing the fabric, apparently a quill and a knife, perhaps the tools of a lawyer or scribe. Next to this symbol is the monogram JT for John Tillot. Papermaking and bookbinding were also carried out at Bury St Edmunds. The Bacton and Worlingworth images show no tools.

The cloth industry

By the 12th and 13th centuries, wool was the source of England's wealth, much of it coming from East Anglia.

Tools of the leather worker as seen at (LEFT TO RIGHT) Rougham, Ixworth, Worlingworth and Badwell Ash.

The area as a whole was noted for its textiles. Shearing, carding, fulling, dyeing, spinning and weaving are all connected to the cloth industry. In the 1550s clothiers were working in such places as Debenham, Badwell Ash and Felsham. The industry had spread from southern Suffolk, centred on Lavenham. At Bury St Edmunds spinning was the only manufacture and it was famed for woollen cloth, but they did not keep up with the fashion for lighter, more colourful fabric.

Stowmarket produced 'tammys' and other Norwich stuffs. Norwich, Ipswich, Colchester, all principal ports of the south-east were busy with the wool trade. Ipswich has twelve medieval parish churches, a few of which have 14th-century flushwork. The highly decorative flint tower of St Lawrence Church only dates from 1882 but below the east window is a medieval stone carving of a pair of draper's shears belonging to John Baldwyn, a benefactor. The nave and chancel were built between 1430 and 1450. There is a woodcarving of a woman using carding brushes at Norton church and a weaver and shearman is recorded at Stowlangtoft because of his misdeeds. Two flushwork symbols on Rougham tower below the battlements appear to be a shuttle for weaving and a loom, both combined with the letter R.

The miller, the farmer and the blacksmith

The rise of the cloth industry brought water-powered fulling mills. Due to the relatively low fall available on Suffolk's rivers, most mills used undershot or low-breastshot wheels. Watermills were also used for corn milling and in the Domesday inventory England had 5,624 watermills recorded. By the late 13th century windmills were becoming commonplace. A badly decayed wheel image appears on Badwell Ash

*Tools of the cloth industry seen at Rougham (*LEFT AND RIGHT*) and Ipswich (*CENTRE*).*

*The blacksmith's
hammer, tongs
and horseshoes
in flushwork at
Badwell Ash.*

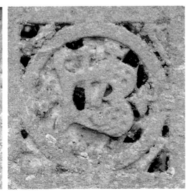

*More tools at
Badwell: for the
farmer (LEFT),
the blacksmith
(CENTRE) and the
miller (RIGHT).*

church together with an almost obliterated image of farming implements. Another millwheel can be seen at Worlingworth church. On the right side of the door at Badwell Ash church there is an unmistakable image of horseshoes and the tools of a blacksmith including an anvil, hammer and tongs; below this an initial B is embellished with hammers.

Guilds and Benefactors

In the mid-1400s the parish and the guild were the two poles around which social and religious life revolved. About 500 guilds have been identified in the county and the majority of parishes in West Suffolk had two or more guilds. The vast majority of records have been lost, especially in Suffolk. These were social and religious guilds. Rural Suffolk had no craft or trade guilds; they were mixed occupational guilds and did not have an emblem to represent a particular occupation like the suburban guilds. Occupations were rarely noted in guild records, so the flushwork devices showing tools of trade were probably donated from individuals who wished their occupations to be known, and in some cases had their initials (monogram) nearby.

Urban guilds (trade guilds) played a different role from those in rural settings. Bury St Edmunds supported at least 30 guilds, Ipswich 15 and Mildenhall 10. Some of these could have been single occupation guilds. One of the universal characteristics of the fraternities was the dedication to a saint or holy event. Some dedications were very commonly chosen by fraternities in certain situations – Holy Trinity or Thomas of Canterbury for merchants' guilds, Corpus Christi for urban government, Catherine and St Nicholas for the Haberdashers, and St John the Baptist for the Merchant Taylors. In Norfolk and Suffolk certain patrons, such as Thomas the Martyr, SS Andrew, Edmund, Margaret, Michael, Mary, Peter and All Saints rose to prominence largely because of the parish dedication but often there were two or more guilds in the same parish. For the honour given by the fraternity, the guild patron (saint) was expected to protect its clients in this life and in

due course to intercede for their souls in purgatory.

Some local guild patrons were St Peter at Bardwell (founded 1440), Jesus and Corpus Christi at Creeting, St Margaret at Thurston, Ixworth and Barningham, St Catherine at Walsham le Willows, St Thomas the Martyr at Cratfield, St John the Baptist at Norton. The Guild of Our Lady was at Woolpit, guilds of the Holy Trinity (1489) and St John the Baptist at St Andrew's at Northwold, and at Needham Market three guilds of St Margaret, the Holy Trinity and St John the Baptist are recorded. St Thomas the Martyr was a very popular saint and many guilds took his name. Dedications to Our Lady or Corpus Christi account for one fifth of Suffolk guilds.

The church base, an annual meeting and a patron saint were the characteristics of a guild and the three main activities were feasting, lightkeeping (maintenance of lights before images of saints and the Blessed Sacrament), and the veneration of saints. (By honouring the saints they encouraged the cult of the saints and promoted purgatory.) The guild undertook a variety of tasks such as money-lending, acting as a benevolent society to the poor and being a source of employment.

Both Norfolk and Suffolk were amongst the most densely populated counties of England in 1377 and by 1515 both were still prosperous, Suffolk emerging as the seventh wealthiest county, with Norfolk not far behind in 12th position (out of 38 counties). Greater personal wealth led to the creation of richer guilds and better-equipped parish churches, although Suffolk guilds were not particularly wealthy. Guilds purchased items for use within the church or the graveyard. Images were commonly owned by guilds. Whilst the guilds provided a number of artefacts, individual guild members were much more active in this area. Naves were furnished almost entirely by private bequests, financed by individuals, chiefly for the good of their souls.

Guild charters were being granted in the 1300s and 1400s, and 1470 onwards was their heyday. Henry VIII dissolved the guilds in 1548 and ordered the destruction of all images of the saints.

Tracery and Mouchettes

A characteristic tendency of the Perpendicular Style of 1330–1530 was to use tracery patterns for covering every spare surface. Tracery is a decorative element designed using a compass that produces complicated geometrical patterns for arches on windows, rose windows and blind windows.

Geometry attempted to understand the workings of God's creation. It encouraged people to think logically instead of relying unquestioningly on received opinions. But in the middle ages a combination of religion and science was often viewed as heresy, and knowledge of geometry was kept secret for fear of reprisals – in a society which could still hang people for sorcery (as late as 1664 in Bury St Edmunds). Geometry features as one of the seven sciences in the

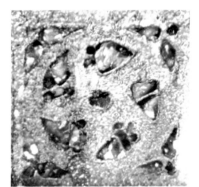

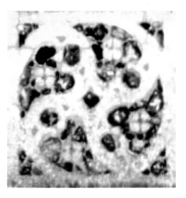

Tracery from Elmswell (LEFT AND CENTRE) *and Ixworth* (RIGHT).

Tracery from (LEFT TO RIGHT) Mendlesham, Rougham and Stratford.

earliest known texts to deal with masonry: the British Library's manuscript Royal 17 A I (a poem dating perhaps from 1390) and Additional Manuscript 23,198 (dating from about 1425–50). Medieval geometers were obsessed with the circle and the square.

The 'mouchette', a curved dagger-shaped tracery motif, was much used in 15th-century Suffolk flushwork. They were set inside a circle which symbolised heaven and eternity. The number and arrangement of the mouchettes in each roundel varies. These

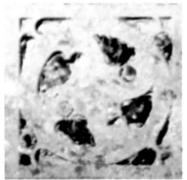

Tracery from (LEFT TO RIGHT) Walsham, Worlingworth and Wortham.

mouchettes may be pure decoration interspersed between the meaningful devices but this is very unlikely as numbers were symbolic in medieval times, often having a complicated meaning that is not always apparent today. Numbers were endowed with occult powers, each number had its divine significance:

1 symbolised God and unity;

2 symbolised the two natures of Christ, the human and the divine;

3 symbolised the Trinity and spiritual wisdom;

4 symbolised the four Evangelists, and the number of elements – all material things – and the Earth;

5 symbolised the five wounds of Christ, and also mankind;

6 symbolised the number of days of creation;

7 was mysterious, and represented the seven deadly sins, or the Holy Spirit, or the seven planets (known at that time), or wisdom;

8 represented new life (many baptismal fonts are octagonal in shape) and the resurrection;

9 symbolised the nine choirs of angels;

10 symbolised the Ten Commandments.

Symmetry and geometry were also given a spiritual significance. Symmetry symbolised inner harmony and geometry was not confined to the narrow meaning it has today: philosophers and theologians used it in a speculative, symbolic and transcendental manner.

These designs appear on at least 12 of the churches reviewed. Several churches have only a few (such as Woolpit, Wortham, Elmswell, Bacton, Badwell Ash and Stratford St Mary). Other churches (such as Ixworth, Northwold, Mendlesham and Worlingworth) have as many as 14. Rougham church has a magnificent rolling frieze on the top of the tower containing 11.

The Chequerboard Motif and The Porch

The chequerboard motif is one of the most common flint images. It appears on at least fourteen churches among other flushwork emblems and it also appears on churches where no other flint motifs exist. Eye church has only one motif which is a chequerboard square which holds the most important position on the tower, the middle front. Rickinghall Superior has the Maria and IHS monograms on the tower and the chequerboard motif at the back of the tower overlooking the main road. Woolpit has approximately 14 chequerboard motifs, one above each of the other flushwork emblems. The number of black or white squares within the motif can be between 2 and 36, and

Chequerboard motifs at (LEFT TO RIGHT) *Cotton, Woolpit and Elmswell.*

it would seem that the number is not significant.

In Christian art the square is the emblem of earth in contrast to heaven. The pattern can be seen on the floor of Westminster Abbey and in the Choir and Chancel at St George's Chapel (begun 1475) at Windsor Castle. During the 1100s it was symbolic for the Knights Templars and later for the Freemasons and can be seen on the floor of their Lodges, sometimes referred to as a 'Moses pavement'. Texts claim that it represents the tiling on which high priests walked in Solomon's temple.

Chequerboard patterns appear in early heraldry, especially in the arms of those who worked for the government. The word 'exchequer' may have derived from the squared cloth used to help in counting money. Barons who collected the state revenues sat at a table covered with a cloth of chessboard design.

Fifteenth-century church porches were often large and elaborate, some containing benches and a stoup and several having an upper floor. The porches were often used for weddings, christenings or civil business for ordinary folk. Many of the churches have a chequered pattern covering the whole of the walls of the porch even on churches where no other flushwork or flint exists. The chequered pattern also covers complete walls on many important medieval civic buildings such as the Guildhalls of Norwich (1407–12) and King's Lynn (1421).

The chequerboard motif can be seen on Elmswell, Hessett, Ixworth, Bacton, Cotton, and Walsham le Willows, Woolpit, Horham, Worlingworth, Eye, Rickinghall Superior, Stratford St Mary and Wortham churches and also on Butley Priory.

A fine chequerboard porch at Woolpit.

Churches of Note

St John the Divine, Elmswell

The chancel of St John's church, Elmswell, was erected about 1300–75 and the tower dates from 1476. Here there are no fewer than 86 flushwork emblems; 34 devices are on the four tower buttresses, 20 large and compound images are at the top of the tower, fifteen along the string course at the base of the tower and a few on the porch.

The symbols are many and varied and include the church year (the Nativity, Epiphany, Easter and Pentecost), kings and saints (St Edward, St Edmund, St

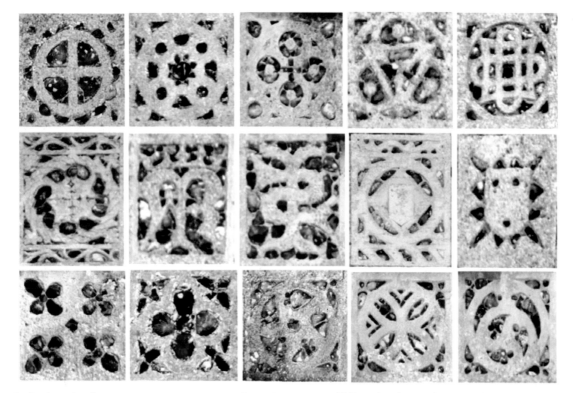

Catherine, St Thomas, St Lawrence, St Stephen, St George and St John), archangels (St Michael), sacred monograms (Christ and Maria), the Trinity, the Star of David, the star of Bethlehem, the sacred heart, a vase and lilies, the chequerboard and several tracery patterns. Elmswell church has the most interesting emblems of all the churches visited and at least twelve are unique to this church. A few similar designs can also be seen on Northwold and Ixworth churches. The flushwork at the top of the tower is badly in need of conservation.

St Mary, Bacton

The nave, chancel and tower of St Mary's, Bacton, were built around 1330 and have no flushwork. The clerestory was added between 1400 and 1500 and it is here that we see 40 flushwork devices, 18 on the south wall and 22 on the north wall, two deep between the windows. Unfortunately the building has had wall supports erected and the ends have partially obscured some of the devices.

The images include the monograms of Christ and St Mary, the cup and viper of St John, St Catherine's wheel with a K above, a chequerboard, the crossed swords for St Paul, three fishes and clover leaves for the Trinity, three more fishes perhaps for St Thomas, the Maltese cross for St John the Baptist, a T for St Thomas of Canterbury, the eight-spoked wheel of life and resurrection, the rose of the Virgin Mary, a triple mitre for the see of Norwich, the letter B, foliage for Lent and Palm Sunday, a bishop's mitre and shield, and the pommée cross of St Michael.

Flushwork at
St Mary's, Bacton,
Suffolk

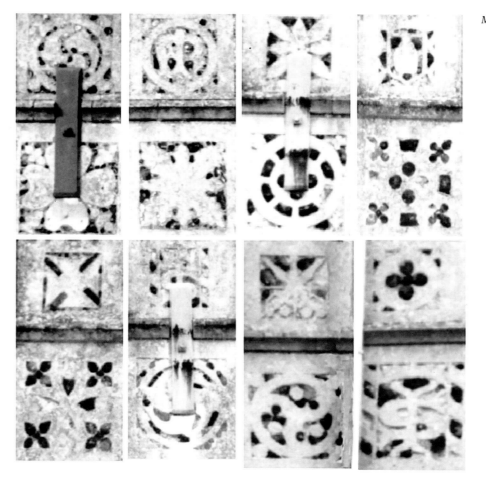

St Mary, Badwell Ash

St Mary's church at Badwell Ash is of the 14th century and the tower is mid-15th-century with the battlements being added about 1480. Here a flushwork inscription reads from the west, 'Pray for the go(o)d Entat (i.e. wellbeing) of jon finchom and margit hys wyfe'. This is a prayer for John and Margaret Fincham in the afterlife.

Flushwork devices decorate the buttresses and a string-course around the tower and porch at ground level. Many flints are now missing and some devices have decayed beyond recognition. The porch has 33 devices and four missing, the four tower buttresses have 12 in all and the string-course has 23 devices. The tower battlements have at least eight devices and an inscription making more than 76 flushwork devices in all.

The designs are particularly interesting and at least four panels show tools of trade. One has blacksmiths' tools with horseshoes and another has a B embellished with hammers. The third device, showing a plough and other farm implements, has lost all its flints. The same fate has happened to the leather-workers' panel showing a stretched and cut skin and four knives. (See pp. 42, 44.)

With the spread of heraldry beyond the circle of knights, the number of arms with tools and implements on them increased. The range included

Badwell Ash: a crowned M for Maria (St Mary), and the Maltese cross of St John the Baptist

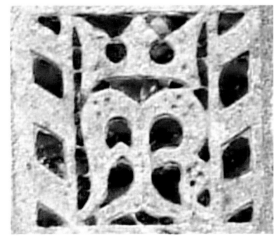

everything from agriculture (ploughshares and whole ploughs) to the tools of small-scale handicrafts. The implements did not only appear in the arms of people who plied a particular trade, but also in the arms and banners of guilds.

Two beautifully designed letters, a W and an R, one at the bottom of each tower buttress, may be a beneficiary's initials but as there is a lack of memorials in the church, the names are not recorded. The top and lower borders of these initials are strikingly similar to the Easter motif on Elmswell Church but appear not to be the same craftsman. (See p. 14.) Other designs are the emblems of St Mary and St John the Baptist, the chalice and host (beside the main door), a crowned T for St Thomas, St Michael the Archangel and the eight-spoked wheel of the resurrection, and the three circles and a triangle of the Trinity.

Holy Trinity, Blythburgh

Henry IV granted the right to rebuild and expand the church at Blythburgh in 1412; it has become

ABOVE *The letters R and W at Badwell Ash*

LEFT *Letters at Blythburgh*

known as the 'Cathedral of the Marshes' owing to its grand proportions. The southern side features roses, quatrefoils, gargoyles, angels and lions in stone. The

only flushwork is low down on the east wall where a row of twelve letters in Lombardic script are boldly set into the flint. The guide states that they are probably the initial letters of a Latin dedication:

Ad Honorem Jesu Beati Sanctae Trinitatis Mariae [et] Sanctae Annae Hic Kancellus Reconstructus [est]:

To the honour of Blessed Jesus, the Holy Trinity, Mary and St Anne this chancel has been rebuilt.

In the middle ages motifs were full of hidden meaning so the letters were probably a reference to the benefactors. At each end of the lettering a pommée cross of St Michael and All Angels has been inserted to keep the benefactors safe in the afterlife. Notice the Trinity shield incorporated into the T panel.

St Andrew's, Cotton

The present church of St Andrew at Cotton dates from the 14th century. The nave was heightened by a clerestory in the 15th century and between the southern clerestory windows are ten designs in flushwork. The images show a chequerboard (unusually containing some half squares), a saints' shield, four quatrefoils for the four evangelists, an eight-spoked wheel of life and a twelve-spoked wheel of the resurrection. Four other designs, peculiar to Cotton church, could represent fire (a star), earth (a square), air (leaves) and water (double chevrons).

All Saints, Hawstead

The tower of Hawstead church was completed around 1510, which is late in the general trend of Suffolk church building. There are heraldic flushwork devices on the tower battlements on the west, north and east sides but none on the south. These images are the heraldry of the benefactors, a cross tau and mullets (five-pointed stars) belonging to the Drury family and the pelicans belong to the Cullum family. The Drury family were resident Lords of the Manor and descendants of the Drurys of Rougham and Thurston. (See p. 39.)

(See p. 39.)

The only other devices are found each side of the west door, a string-course with five images each side. The Drury mullet appears next to a wool weight

LEFT *Hawstead*

OPPOSITE PAGE *Cotton*

Hawstead

and also next to a square frame wrapped with loops (wool?). An hourglass and a Star of David signify temperance and charity and the quatrefoil for Christianity.

St Mary the Virgin, Ixworth

St Mary's church at Ixworth was enlarged and remodelled during the late 15th century; several Ixworth people made bequests in their wills for the new tower around 1472. There are 66 flushwork emblems on Ixworth church, six on each side of the

tower battlements and a total of 32 on the tower buttresses and ten on the string-course at ground level. One device at the lower part of the tower buttress bears the crown and arrows saltire of St Edmund and has the words 'Mast Robert Schot Abot'. Robert Schot was Abbot at Bury St Edmunds from 1472 to 1474. Four symbols underneath each other on the buttress facing the road are a T for St Thomas, a rose for St Mary, a crowned IHS for Christ and a crown and arrows for St Edmund. Other designs include the E for St Edward, the wheel for St Catherine, a

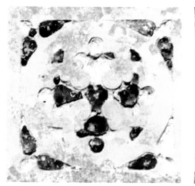

crowned M for St Mary, an elaborate intertwined IHS for Christ, tools of the leather trade (see p. 42), and lozenges. In addition there are 18 tracery designs with varying numbers and arrangements of mouchettes. It would be worth comparing some of the designs with Elmswell and Northwold churches as several designs are very similar and are not found elsewhere.

St Andrew's, Northwold

St Andrew's church at Northwold in Norfolk is 12 miles north-west of Thetford. It has more flushwork emblems than any other church and some of the designs have striking similarities to those on Ixworth and Elmswell churches in Suffolk. All three churches had connections with the Abbey at Bury St Edmunds, and the masons could have been the same craftsmen.

St Andrew's has a very high tower dating from about 1480 with four emblems around the tower battle-

Northwold

ments, 20 on each of the two tower buttresses at the west end, and 17 and 16 on the east buttresses, plus 21 on a stringcourse around the west door, making 98 emblems in all. There were probably several more on the east buttresses but some have been covered when the roof was heightened.

There is a fascinating variety of designs, hardly any two alike. The meaning of some has yet to be interpreted; other are obvious, and mostly religious. Motifs which can be seen in other sections of this book include those of St Andrew, St Audrey, St Lawrence, St Stephen, St Michael and St Thomas, as well as the Mystic Rose, the fleur de lys, the monogram of Maria and the shield of the Trinity. There are also a saint's shield, mouchettes, a shield with five circles representing the five wounds of Christ, and the ring of Innocent.

Ring of Innocent – Four Rings

The story goes that in May of the year 1205, Pope Innocent III sent the king of England a set of four golden rings, each set with a variety of precious stones. Innocent explained that the rings had particular symbolic significance: the circular form was to represent eternity, the number four was to signify the four virtues that make up the constancy of mind – justice, fortitude, prudence and temperance. The gemstones themselves were also endowed with meaning: the green emerald representing faith, the blue sapphire, hope, the red garnet, charity, and the bright topaz, good works.

St Nicholas Church, Rattlesden

Rattlesden is one of only two churches (the other being Stratford St Mary) with a theme running through the flushwork devices. If all the churches reviewed had a set theme my research would have been considerably easier.

There was a church in Rattlesden in 1086 that was rebuilt in the 13th century. Major remodelling took place in the 15th century – wills dated 1473 mention bequests for glazing and the nave roof was heightened in 1480–84. The embattled southern parapet with the devices in flushwork probably dates from this time.

The images represent the eleven apostles, St Paul, St Edmund (King of the East Angles) the sacred monograms of Jesus and Mary, and St Etheldreda. Working from west to east they represent:

St James the Less – J

St Philip – P

St Thaddeus (St Jude) – T

St Bartholomew – B

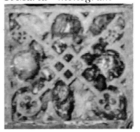

*St Edmund
– crown and arrows*

*St Matthew
– the letter M*

*St Peter – crossed keys
St Maria – monogram*

Jesus – sacred monogram

St John – a dragon

*St Thomas
– three fishes, letter T*

*St Etheldreda (St Audrey)
– letter A with crown*

*Medieval Flushwork
of East Anglia*

63

St Paul – crossed swords

St James – scallop shells

St Andrew – A

St Simon – a reversed S

On the west parapet are the arms of the Chamberlain and Bourchier families (see page 37) and on the eastern parapet are the mitre and crossed croziers of Hervey, Bishop of Ely 1109–31.

Stratford St Mary

At Stratford St Mary the list of rectors begins AD 1312. Thomas Mors, a wealthy cloth merchant, added the north aisle of this church in 1499. The outside of this part of the church has flushwork devices that were obviously designed to show off the generosity and piety of the benefactor.

Below window level, stretching the whole length of the church in large letters, is a Latin inscription which means 'Pray for the souls of Thomas Mors and Margaret his wife who caused this aisle to be erected in the year of our Lord 1499'.

part of
'Jesus is my love'

part of the
alphabet.

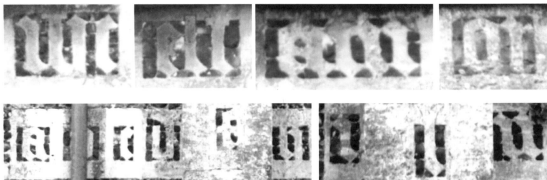

The eastern part of the aisle, which was built in 1530 by their descendants, has more large lettering and reads in English 'Pray for the soullys of Edward Mors and Alys his wyf and all crysten sowlys Anno Domini 1530'.

On the top of each buttress appear the letters 'IHS EST AMOR MEUS' ('Jesus is my love').

Along the centre of the wall between the windows is a complete alphabet (the letters J and U are absent because at that date the letters I/J and U/V had not

yet been separated into different letters). As this part of the building is very near the road the alphabet could be easily memorised by the regular passers by.

Below the alphabet, interspersed among various ornamental devices, are the letters PBAES which according to the church guide represents the prayer 'Propitiemini beati ad eternam salutem' (Be propitious, ye blessed ones, to eternal salvation).

Other devices include the crowned T for St Thomas, the crowned M for Maria and the St John symbol. St John always appeared on rood screens of that period and in flushwork is usually situated next to Mary. These three devices are situated above the inscription as if requesting the saints to intercede for the dead. There is also a chequerboard, a couple of mouchette roundels and several merchants' marks belonging to Thomas Mors. (See p. 41 .)

*Motifs at Rougham:
grapes, possibly
representing
the wine trade,
alongside the tools
of trade of the
clothier.*

St Mary, Rougham

St Mary's Church at Rougham was rebuilt in the 14th century and the great west tower was added in the 15th century. The only flushwork is at the top of the tower, which has a most elaborate and extremely complicated flintwork design stretching between the four corner buttresses on each side. There are 24 different circular motifs joined by a rolling line, making a frieze that appears mostly decorative except for a communion cup and wafer at the far end. Incorporated into this frieze are the overlapping letters JD and JT representing the benefactors, John Drury and John Tillot. According to the monuments and brasses, the wealthy and important family of Drury had lived in Rougham for nearly 200 years and John Drury's father Roger was a knight, so it is no wonder that money was available for this beautifully artistic and unique piece of architecture.

Above the flushwork frieze are central panels with the inscriptions 'pray for Drury' on the north side and 'pray for the sowle of John Tillot' on the south side. On the east battlement the central panel has the crowned monogram of Mary incorporating two pots with lilies. The west battlement central panel is divided into four, showing again the monograms JT for John Tillot and JD for John Drury and beside these are their trade tools, the instruments that created their wealth (see p. 43). These flushwork panels are some of the largest in Suffolk.

The large symbol of grapes standing alone to the left of the tools of trade and monograms could reflect the benefactor's trade in wine.

St Mary, Walsham le Willows

St Mary's church at Walsham le Willows was in the care of the canons of Ixworth priory until 1534.

The church dates from the 14th century and the porch is 15th-century. The north face of the porch is covered with lozenge patterned flushwork which is also seen on a bold string-course at ground level on the north aisle. The clerestory was added about 1465, and between the clerestory windows are 17 flushwork devices on the north side and 17 on the south side. The

devices include the monograms of Christ and St Mary, Lent foliage, the rose of the Virgin Mary, the eight-spoked wheel of life and resurrection, a saint's shield, a two-lozenged panel, several roundels with various numbers of mouchettes and a Catherine wheel. The guild chapel of St Catherine was in the south aisle in medieval times.

The sign of eight spokes around a hub was worn by medieval knights and was said to help overcome spiritual frailties.

*Wheels in flushwork
at St Mary's,
Walsham-le-Willows*

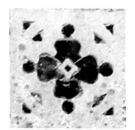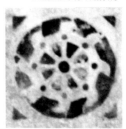

St Mary, Woolpit

Woolpit is a well-kept and pretty village which has a magnificent church. The Shrine of Our Lady of Woolpit was a famous healing well and a place of pilgrimage throughout the middle ages.

The oldest part of the church was built about 1200, the south aisle is 14th-century and the north aisle is mid-15th-century. Between the clerestory windows on both aisles we find the flushwork devices, about 14 in all, each one under a chequered square of flushwork. The magnificent stone carved and chequered porch, built about 1439 (see p. 49), and spire of 1853 overshadow the flushwork devices which appear quite

insignificant in comparison. The designs include the sacred monograms, St Catherine's wheel and three other wheels, one with inner and outer spikes (flames?) which could be the wheel of the Ascension.

St Mary, Worlingworth

St Mary's church chancel at Worlingworth was built about 1280–1310 and the western tower and south porch were added about 1460.

Many flushwork motifs can be seen on the nave buttresses and on the string-course at ground level around the door. All around the nave at waist level are empty saints' shields. The other devices include

Flushwork devices at St Mary's, Woolpit

 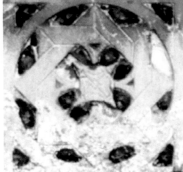 

the letter e for St Edward the Confessor, the chequer-board, the Maria monogram, the IHC monogram, the chalice and host of the Blessed Sacrament, the lily of the Virgin Mary, the St John emblem, a K for St Catherine, the rose of the Virgin Mary and the pommée cross of St Michael. There are two suns, one containing Christ's monogram (the sign that appeared to St Bernardino of Siena). There are also many roundels with varying numbers of mouchettes.

A saint's shield (*above left*) has rays around the edge that distinguishes it from an heraldic shield. These are seen on Rattlesden church, Northwold church, Elmswell, Walsham le Willows, Hessett and Wortham churches. These were possibly a tribute to all the saints so that no one of them would be left out, as medieval people were very superstitious.

Compare the two flushwork panels (*below*) from Worlingworth and Elmswell: the number of circles in both is 25. The number must have some significance, for the churches are over 20 miles apart and the craftsmen don't appear to be the same for both churches.

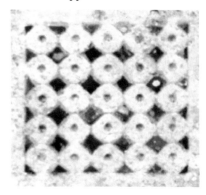 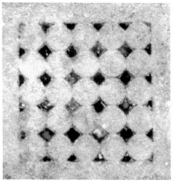

Emblems at
Worlingworth

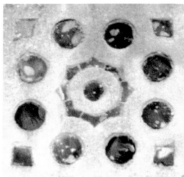

Fornham All Saints

The south aisle of Fornham All Saints church was added in the late 15th century and it is here on the embattled parapet that we see 12 flushwork panels. The images include the M for St Mary, followed by a K for St Katherine and then Christ's monogram. The next three panels spell 'Lord have mercy' (see p. 40). Other panels show the letters A, R and D, a T for St Thomas and an E for St Edmund. St

Fornham: E for St
Edmund, tied to
a tree

Edmund, King of the East Angles, was supposedly tied to a tree and shot at by the Danes. Look carefully at the E, which appears to be tied to the wreath.

St Mary, Grundisburgh

The clerestory of St Mary's church at Grundisburgh was erected about 1418 and between the clerestory windows there are 12 flushwork panels. At the west end are the crown and arrows of St Edmund, the arms of the Tudenham family, a letter T and a vase and lily (see p. 36). The following six panels contain crowns above the letters AVE MARIA (see p. 34) and the east panels show an A and Christ's monogram.

The embattled parapet has a stone-carved merchant's mark of the benefactor Thomas Wall and the Salters' arms (not shown in this book, but see p. 41).

St Ethelbert, Hessett

Hessett church (rebuilt 1450–1500) has only a few flushwork devices along the base near the porch. One or two have been insensitively patched up with cement. The images include a saint's shield, foliage, a gridiron and a monogram for John Bacon (who died in 1513 and is thought to have been a benefactor). The Bacon families were Lords of the Manor of Hessett.

St Mary, Horham

Horham tower was built or rebuilt about 1499–1513. The flushwork panels on the tower parapet show the monograms of Christ, St Mary and St John and two chequerboard panels. Carved stone shields beneath the tower battlements show the chalice and wafer of the Holy Communion and the arms of local families surrounded by decorative flintwork.

St Mary, Mendlesham

St Mary's church at Mendlesham dates from the 1200s but the tower is 15th-century. The flushwork and carved stonework panels are on a string-course at ground level around the tower and most of these are in a bad state of decay. There are 27 flint panels and six carved stone panels; of these at least 14 are tracery patterns, surprisingly all different. In addition there

is a 12-spoked wheel and the St Mary and St Thomas symbols.

St Martin, New Buckenham

St Martin's, New Buckenham, Norfolk, was rebuilt between 1479 and 1530. Its flintwork is very similar to that of St Mary's at Mendlesham in Suffolk. There are many non-flint devices on a long string-course at ground level and panels of flushwork on the tower buttresses. Symbols include St Mary, St Thomas and the chequerboard.

St Andrew, South Lopham

Originally the South Lopham church was dedicated to St Nicholas and between 1460 and 1480 the nave was heightened and given a clerestory. The flushwork panels between the clerestory windows show bold crowned letters of saints and benefactors.

St Mary the Virgin, Wortham

The clerestory was added to Wortham church about 1410 and between the clerestory windows in sets of two and three we see approximately 19 flushwork panels. The images include the St Catherine's wheel, the wheel of life between St Michael's pommée cross and the All Saints shield, the chequerboard, the rose of the Virgin Mary next to the Maltese cross of John the Baptist, four squares representing earth and several roundels containing mouchettes. There is also the St Mary symbol between two different representations of Christ's monogram. Four other flint panels show the letters STSM with a small *a* in the corner of the S panels; these letters stand for SANCTA TRINITAS SANCTA MARIA.

St Nicholas, Feltwell

At Feltwell, Norfolk, there are six 15th-century panels, two spelling the words Thomas Deye, who was probably one of the church benefactors.

Church of the Assumption of the Blessed Virgin Mary, Redenhall

Redenhall Church has large flushwork devices on the top of the tower. These appear to be abstract and are mostly based on the number eight, the number for new life. There are 64 circles on one panel, eight squares within squares in another, and a panel with four crosses along the top and sides, and several wheels containing either eight spokes or eight elements.

Panels commemorating Thomas Deye at Feltwell

Bibliography

Frederick Armitage, *The Old Guilds of England* (London: Weare, 1918)

Udo Becker, *The Continuum Encyclopedia of Symbols* (London: Continuum, 2000)

James Bentley, *A Calendar of Saints: The Lives of the Principal Saints of the Christian Year* (London: Orbis, 1987)

Marc Drogin, *Medieval Calligraphy: Its History and Technique* (London: Prior, 1980; Constable, 1989)

David Dymond and Edward Martin (eds), *An Historical Atlas of Suffolk* (Ipswich: Suffolk County Council Planning Department, 1988; rev. ed. Suffolk County Council Archaeology Service, 1999)

David Dymond and Peter Northeast, *A History of Suffolk* (Chichester: Phillimore, 1985; rev. ed. 1995)

David High Farmer, *The Oxford Dictionary of Saints* (Oxford: Clarendon Press, 1978; 5th ed. Oxford University Press, 2003)

Ken Farnhill, *Guilds and the Parish Community in Late Medieval East Anglia, c. 1470–1550* (York: York Medieval Press, 2001)

George Ferguson, *Signs and Symbols in Christian Art* (New York: Oxford University Press, 1954; 2nd ed. London: Zwemmer, 1955)

F. A. Girling, *English Merchants' Marks: A Field Survey of Marks Made by Merchants and Tradesmen in*

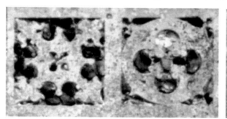

England Between 1400 and 1700 (London: Lion & Unicorn Press, 1962; Oxford University Press, 1964)

Stephen Hart, *Flint Architecture of East Anglia* (London: Giles de la Mare, 1999)

W. Ellwood Post, *Saints, Signs and Symbols* (London: SPCK, 1964; 2nd ed. 1975)

Church Guides

Bacton
Badwell Ash (Brian Turner)
Blythburgh (Hugh Roberts, Mary Montague and
    Barry Naylor)
Butley Priory (Sheila Harrison)
Cotton (Roy Tricker)
Gipping Chapel (W. H. Sewell)
Grundisburgh (Roy Tricker)
Hawstead (A. E. Hillman)
Hessett (Roy Tricker)
Horham (John Harvey and David Streeter)
Ixworth (Sylvia Colman)
South Lopham
Mendlesham (Philip Gray)
Rattlesden (Roy Tricker)
Rougham (Stratford St Mary)
Walsham le Willows
Woolpit
Worlingworth (Roy Tricker)
Wortham (Westray)

A special thank you to all the anonymous authors and photographers who have contributed to these guides.

This decorative cross is the only flushwork symbol in Felsham church.

Index